TOP 10 FASTEST

Boats

SHERRY HOWARD

Rourke Educational Media
A Division of Carson Dellosa Education
rourkeeducationalmedia.com

ROURKE'S
SCHOOL to HOME
CONNECTIONS

BEFORE AND DURING READING ACTIVITIES

Before Reading: *Building Background Knowledge and Vocabulary*

Building background knowledge can help children process new information and build upon what they already know. Before reading a book, it is important to tap into what children already know about the topic. This will help them develop their vocabulary and increase their reading comprehension.

Questions and Activities to Build Background Knowledge:

1. Look at the front cover of the book and read the title. What do you think this book will be about?
2. What do you already know about this topic?
3. Take a book walk and skim the pages. Look at the table of contents, photographs, captions, and bold words. Did these text features give you any information or predictions about what you will read in this book?

Vocabulary: *Vocabulary Is Key to Reading Comprehension*

Use the following directions to prompt a conversation about each word.

- Read the vocabulary words.
- What comes to mind when you see each word?
- What do you think each word means?

Vocabulary Words:

- *catamaran*
- *draft*
- *eco-friendly*
- *hydroplanes*
- *propel*
- *vessel*

During Reading: *Reading for Meaning and Understanding*

To achieve deep comprehension of a book, children are encouraged to use close reading strategies. During reading, it is important to have children stop and make connections. These connections result in deeper analysis and understanding of a book.

Close Reading a Text

During reading, have children stop and talk about the following:

- Any confusing parts
- Any unknown words
- Text to text, text to self, text to world connections
- The main idea in each chapter or heading

Encourage children to use context clues to determine the meaning of any unknown words. These strategies will help children learn to analyze the text more thoroughly as they read.

When you are finished reading this book, turn to the next-to-last page for **After Reading Questions** and an **Activity**.

Table of Contents

Full Speed Ahead

Have you tried running through water? Moving fast through water is hard work.

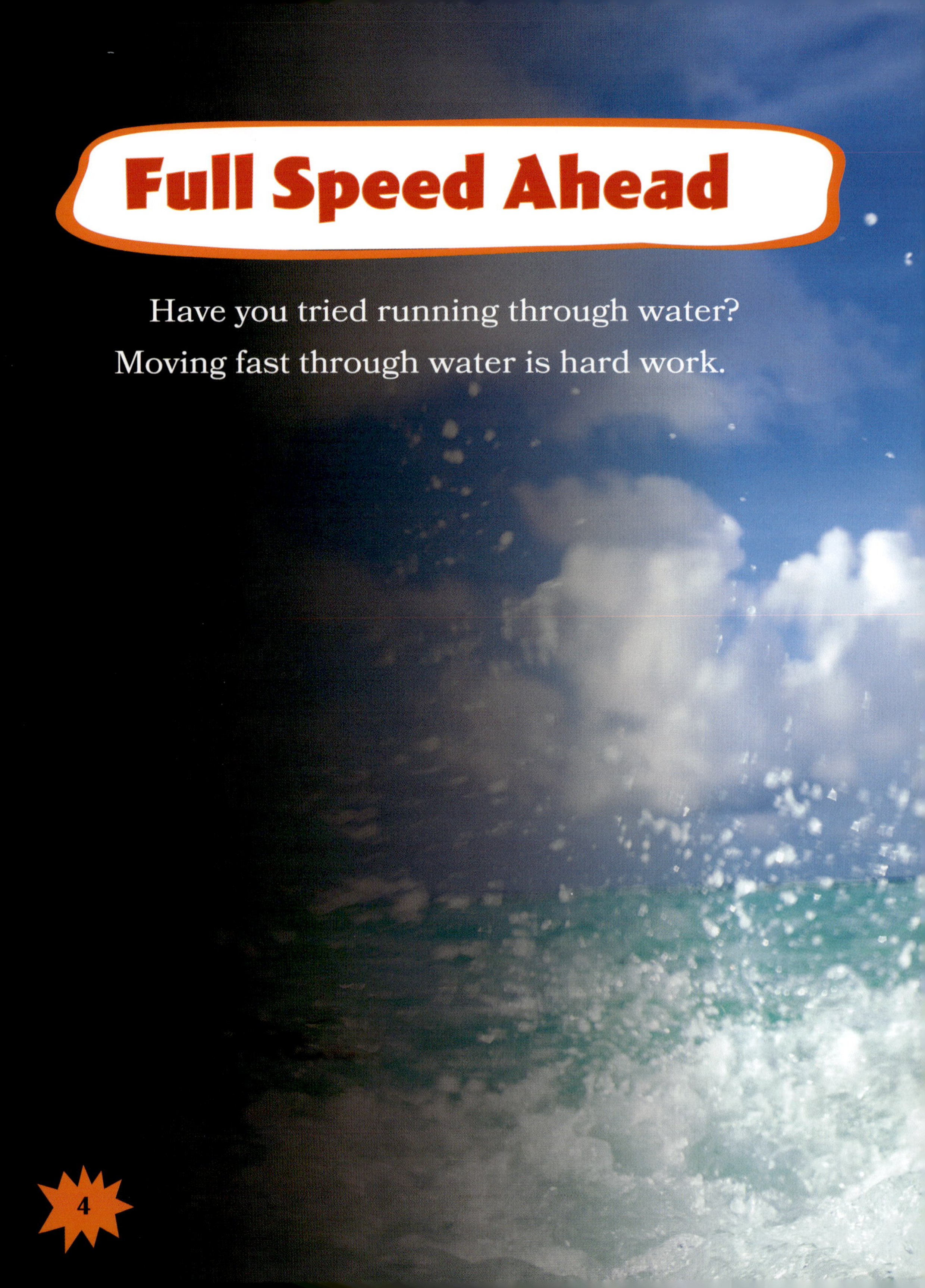

But many boats are built for speed. Some are built for super speed!

Bluebird K7

This boat was one of the first turbine **hydroplanes**. It earned seven speed records in the 1950s and 1960s.

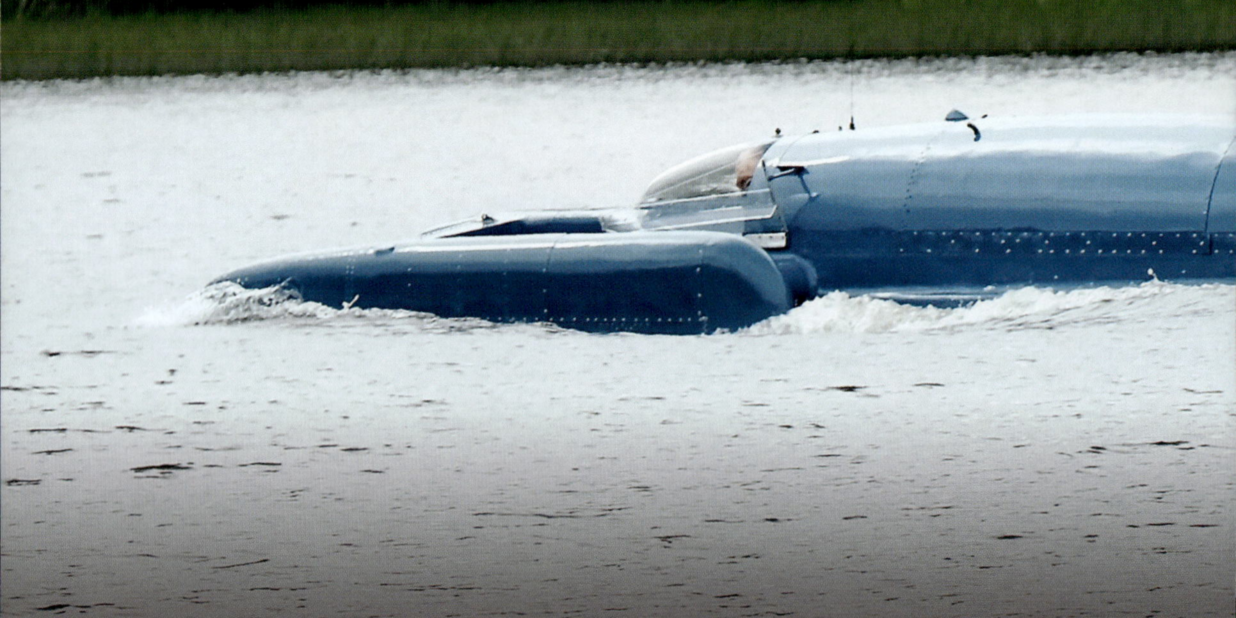

10 **hydroplanes** (HYE-droh-playns): fast, light motorboats designed to skim over the water's surface

The pilot tried to break his own speed record. The boat flipped. It burst into flames. The pilot died.

H1 Unlimited

Hydroplanes of this type look like drag-racing cars. They race at speeds over 200 miles (322 kilometers) per hour. That is crazy fast!

GRAHAM
TRUCKING, INC.
GRAHAM
DYC

A-Class Catamaran

Racing boats in this class are made from high-tech materials such as carbon fiber. **Catamaran** means "logs tied together."

catamaran (kat-uh-muh-RAN): a boat with two joined hulls

Vestas Sailrocket 2

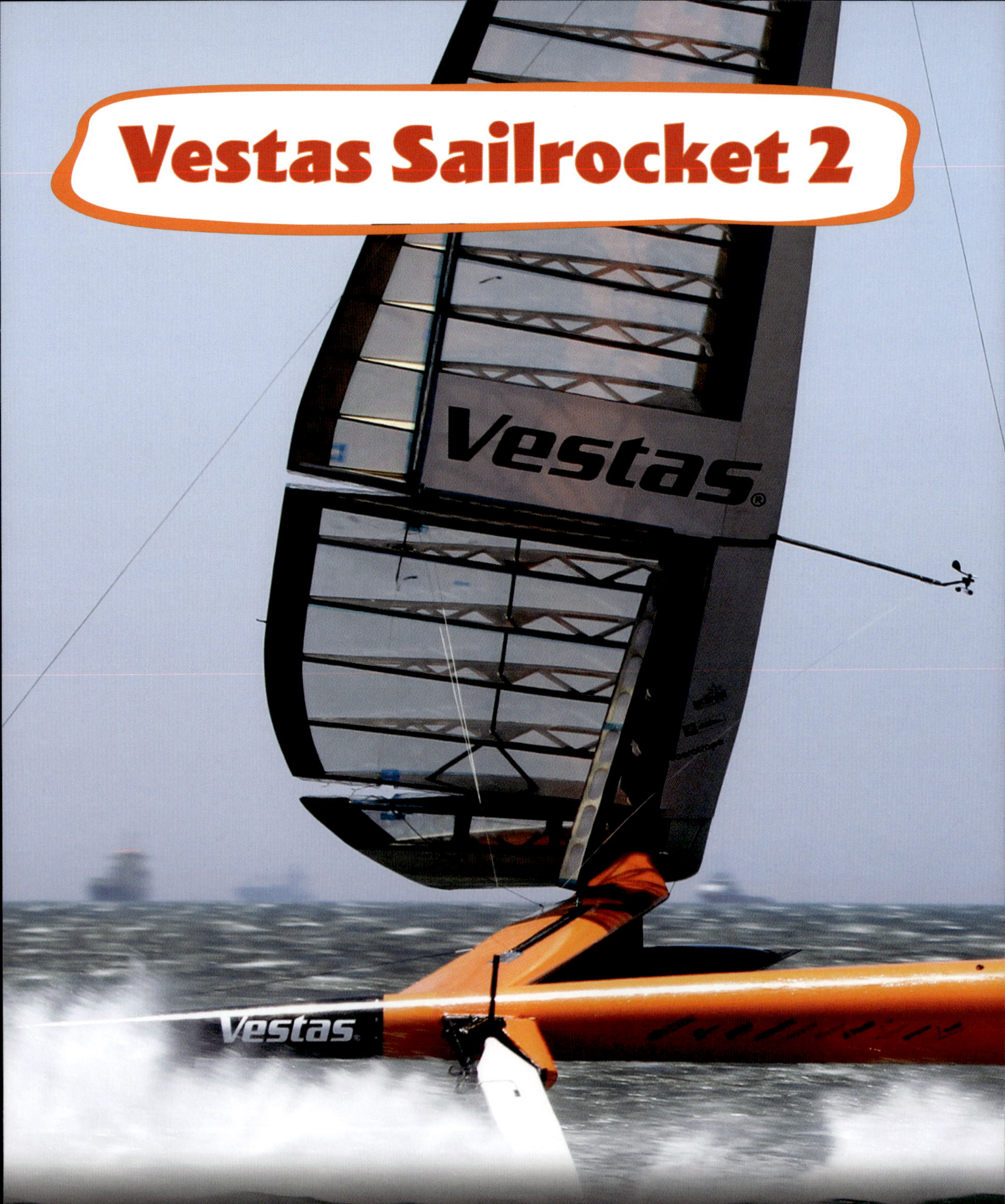

10 **vessel** (VES-uhl): a boat or ship

This **vessel** looks like a rocket with a sail. It does not have an engine. Its design makes it the fastest sailboat in the world.

U.S. Navy M80 Stiletto

This speedy military boat tests new technology. It has a shallow **draft** of just three feet (0.9 meters). Drones can land on the top.

draft (draft): on a boat, the distance between the surface of the water and the deepest part of the hull

Cigarette AMG Electric Drive

Daimler AG

This boat is **eco-friendly**. A dozen electric engines blast it across the water. It is faster than a speeding car!

eco-friendly (EE-koh-frend-lee): not harmful to the environment

Earthrace

This unusual boat set a world record. It went around the world in 60 days, 23 hours, and 49 minutes.

Spirit of Australia

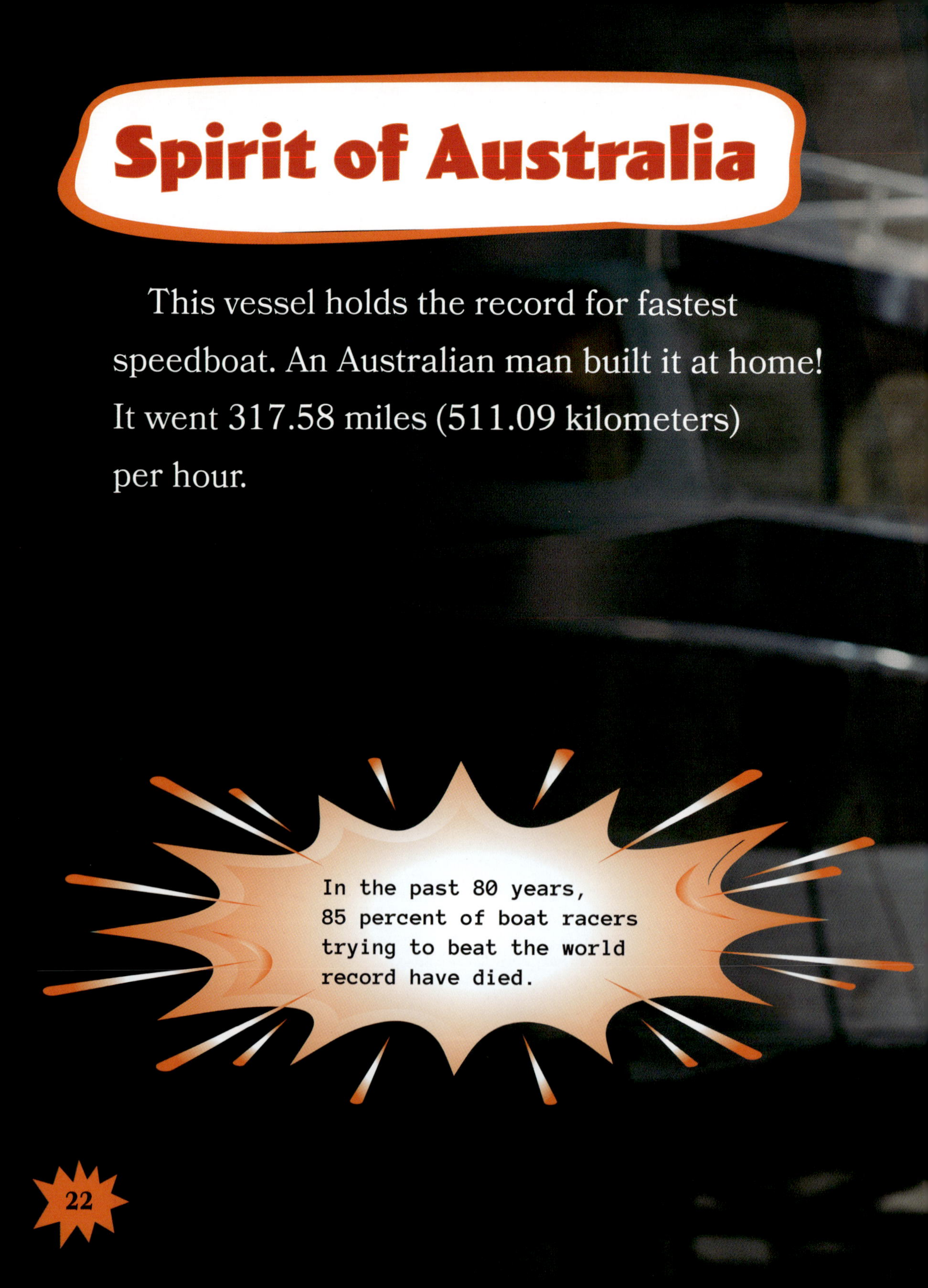

This vessel holds the record for fastest speedboat. An Australian man built it at home! It went 317.58 miles (511.09 kilometers) per hour.

In the past 80 years, 85 percent of boat racers trying to beat the world record have died.

Mystic C5000-R

This is the fastest speedboat you can buy. It can go 240 miles (386 kilometers) per hour. It sells for about one million dollars!

QATAR
26

Buster Phantom

This boat is made of aluminum. Twin engines **propel** it through the water at high speeds. It comes with grab bars for five passengers!

propel (pruh-PEL): to push something forward

Leena

High speed on the water is dangerous. A swell can make a boat flip. A quick turn can cause a crash. Racers risk their lives in the world's fastest boats.

Memory Game

Look at the pictures. What do you remember reading on the pages where each image appeared?

Index

After Reading Questions

1. What is the fastest speedboat someone can buy?
2. What are some dangers speedboat racers face?
3. Which boat is eco-friendly?
4. Where was the fastest known speed boat built?
5. Which boat looks like a rocket with a sail?

Activity

Which boat discussed in the book interested you most? Using books or the internet, research that boat further. What more can you learn about the way the boat is built for speed? Write a story about taking a ride on that boat.

About the Author

Sherry Howard loves to learn about fast boats. She once rode on a huge speedboat called the Screamer. She screamed the whole time!

www.rourkeeducationalmedia.com

PHOTO CREDITS: Cover & Title Pg ©oariff; Pg 16 & 30 ©U.S. Navy, Photographer's Mate Airman Damien Horvath; Pg 18 & 30 ©Daimler AG - Global Communications Mercedes-Benz Cars; Pg 20 & 30 ©David Castor @ wiki; Pg 24 & 30 ©JAY NICHOLS; Pg 26 & 30 ©Mikasarkijarvi @ wiki; Pg 8 & 30 ©Iain Cochrane; Pg 4 ©CasarsaGuru; Pg 6 ©kirza; Pg 10 ©Darren Brode; Pg 12 ©Yetanotheraccount1 @ wiki; Pg 14 ©Helena Darvelid Sailrocket; Pg 23 ©shironosov; Pg 28 ©Tim Allen

Edited by: Kim Thompson
Cover and Interior design by: Kathy Walsh

Library of Congress PCN Data

Boats / Sherry Howard
(Top Ten Fastest)
ISBN 978-1-73161-460-5 (hardcover)
ISBN 978-1-73161-261-8 (soft cover)
ISBN 978-1-73161-565-7 (e-Book)
ISBN 978-1-73161-670-8 (ePub)
Library of Congress Control Number: 2019932356

Rourke Educational Media
Printed in the United States of America,
North Mankato, Minnesota